THE BRIEF REINCARNATION OF A GIRL

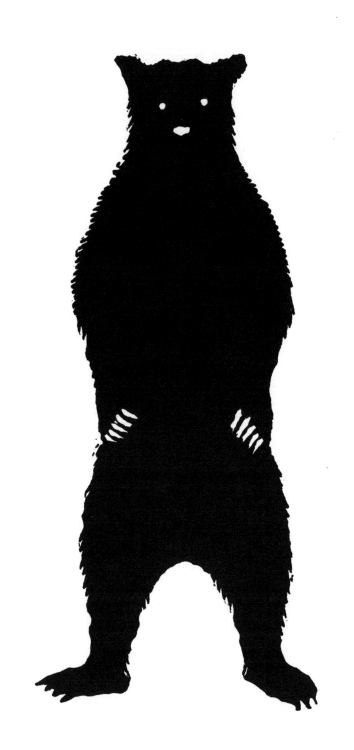

The Brief Reincarnation of a Girl

SUE GOYETTE

★

GASPEREAU PRESS LIMITED
PRINTERS & PUBLISHERS
KENTVILLE, NS
MMXV

Logic! Good gracious! What rubbish!
E. M. FORSTER

I

The girl refused to be afraid when she climbed
on high things. Her mother shaved the legs of the furniture
and, along with some cough syrup, stewed it
with a few of the girl's father's beer caps. The girl spit
a whole parade's worth of bicycle bells back at her
and pranced around in her diaper. The mother sat in the closet,
lit a candle, and located the doctor with binoculars.
The doctor, appearing as a bathrobe, urged
the mother to slap the girl with her slippers then take her
pulse. The girl had begun to growl which was upsetting
the cats. The mother upped the dosage of bottle caps
and added some baby Aspirin. The doctor suggested
more conventional medication, the girl sounded bipolar
and should be on a leash. What they didn't know
was that the girl had collected enough stickers
to reward the universe. She had a blanket and a bear.
She had resolved that when she got up from the floor
that last time, she'd be in another time zone
with better tasting furniture and a door that closed.

The mother sat in the closet and trained her binoculars
on the doctor's prescription pad. They were trying their hand
at automatic writing. The doctor wrote *Chevrolet*
and *hubcaps*. The mother wrote *she's driving me crazy*.
The doctor discussed the dosage and they both agreed,
given the century and the 24-hour drugstore, they could treat themselves
to a chocolate bar and maybe a slurpee. The mother wondered
if there was a pill for the minutes before the girl's father
got home. Are the minutes filled with knives or cement?
the doctor wanted to know. Sometimes knives and sometimes
cigarette burns. If the bath was filled, the doctor wanted
to know, would the water be hot or cold? The mother
complained that she didn't have time for a bath because her daughter
often would stand on her dresser and pronounce that she was
a burglar. Was she armed? the doctor wanted to know.
The doctor reminded the mother to put a colander against
her daughter's chest and strain her heartbeats. The mother
wondered if she was qualified to own a colander. They laughed
when they both wrote down parenting with a sad face.
The doctor urged the mother to draw happy faces instead. A whole
page of them and then to swallow four of them a day.
Maybe, the mother said jovially, one day, the father and the girl
just wouldn't come home.

Her prescription pad was important to the doctor.
She'd check it during meals with friends
and they'd complain that her attention
was elsewhere. It rode in her car like a lap dog
on the passenger seat and she'd slide it across
her kitchen counter when she got home as if she was
in a tournament and her opponent was verging on
winning. Her prescription pad was her compact mirror
that she'd check her reflection in for signs of success.
She was managing so many cases with it, it was part remote
control, part garage door opener, part smartphone.
Often she'd write out the same dosage and the same medication
for mostly two and three-year-olds. This was the part of her job
she was growing bitter about. One day, to shake things up,
she prescribed a stapler to a mother and added a filing cabinet
for all of her complaints. She once, notoriously, prescribed
a shot of hurricane to a recovering umbrella. It is still unbelievable to her
that her office is so small. There isn't even room for a feather,
for example, to measure her soul and the truth of how good
she looks in heels. It was imperative to the doctor that the clothes
she wore to court coordinated with her prescription pad.

The girl's father had been prescribed aluminum foil. After
the charges and the fallen tree, the dosage was increased
and a roasting pan was added to his treatment with a stiff barbeque
brush. He had broken his addiction to his watch and was rarely
present at his appointments. The doctor would try contacting
him using her own father's slipper and the window facing
west in her office but he was often unplugged, traipsing
through his excuses and fondling park benches and pigeons.
The problem was his children had become aquariums
of swimming pills. Which, as far as he could see, wasn't
a problem. The other problem was that he had laughed
the same morning his daughter had been found dead.
He wasn't laughing at her, he claimed in court, he was laughing
at the way he had taken a frying pan by mistake
and was feeling the repercussions of having taken the wrong
medication. If he had taken the table lamp and three of the apologies
the doctor had prescribed, she may still be alive
and wearing the higher dose of her crown.

The lawyer prayed for a parking space.
If he could get a parking space he wouldn't be
late. He called upon his mother
who had died of lung cancer
three years before to grant him
a parking spot. He knew he was often
late and had miscalculated the five minutes
he'd given himself for an actual vacation hour
that seemed to stretch into a beach
and at least two drinks. He knew better
than to do that again, he promised,
but if his mother could find him a parking spot
he'd really be able to breathe.

The doctor, on hearing how panicked the lawyer
had been looking for a parking spot, immediately
prescribed him a clock and a drink which he drank
right away. He set the clock back to being on time
and the deliberations began over whether the mother
had realized the child couldn't pronounce her words
because she was two or if the child was dysarthric
and clearly a combined case of bipolar and ADHD,
committed to continually hiding the remote
and talking her gibberish while important things were happening
on the mother's television show. In short: committed to drive her mother
crazy. The jury was hungry. They'd been promised
croissants, a luxury, and had only got bagels
without cream cheese. The doctor prescribed them donuts
and a referee whistle which they used when they didn't
understand something being said. The lawyer, for example,
had to explain why he was still talking when all of their stomachs
told them it was time for a break.

The girl's mother, without telling the doctor, had taken
double her dose of television and had neglected
to take any of her patience. She, just this minute,
had remembered that she had other children.
They were wan and so prescribed a tanning bed
and a baseball bat to beat off the curve ball
of their father's hands. The boy would often say
he was a lion and had been prescribed a cage and a zoo.
The sister didn't see him after that and missed the way
his tail would give him away. She was prescribed a journal
and a blind for her window. Her father would often try to convince her
that he was the cape she'd been waiting for and would try
to dress her for a dance he insisted she'd be gowned for.
This is when she missed her brother the most. Not for his company,
but for his claws. The judge kept pounding his gavel,
yelling *order* which upset the mother because it reminded her
of the paramedic who'd broken down the door of her own father's
house when someone on their street had called the ambulance
because they couldn't think of what else to do.

Each child was paired with a songbird and a blanket,
the daycare teacher told the court. The girl often insisted
on singing longer than they had time for so she understood
the prescribed muzzle—in a way. The girl would often
help another child attain the height they were after
with their blocks by climbing on a chair and crowning
the building with a triangle. Objection, one of the lawyers
yelled, and the juror whose father had also yelled felt faint
and took her prescribed sunflower seed to calm the furnace that
rumbled on in her stomach. The daycare teacher clapped her one,
two, three-three, four clap and all the young children
still camping out in the adults in the courtroom stopped
what they were doing to listen. Her job, she said in a skipping rope
voice, her job was to protect the joy of childhood
and she did not see anything wrong with allowing the girl
to be the tree she insisted on being. The juror on sunflower seeds
wasn't sure whether the daycare teacher had just said tree
or truck. Her saliva, she noticed, was starting to taste
like a bridge token.

The doctor had to prescribe herself
a daydream after the drudgery of the morning
in court. She injected it into her thigh in the women's
bathroom and slumped against the wall. And then she was
approaching a podium and accepting a housemaid
and a bouquet of parrots. It was the highest order,
she was told. Her research on the impact of dust
in a child's environment and their mental health
has changed the way childhood is medicated.
She had a prepared speech in her clutch
as well as a strand of pearls and a parking ticket.
The next thing she knew, she was putting her hands
in a Dyson hand dryer and adjusting her lipstick
in a painting that looked so much like her, she nodded
approval. She assumed it was her house key ringing in her purse,
so she didn't bother answering it. Recess, they had called
this break, almost to spite her with the image of a building
spewing out more children than should be possible.

The mother was trying to get the doctor's attention.
She needed a pencil and was wondering if she could get one
prescribed. Her wrist was tired from cashing cheques
in her dream last night. She had cashed one with so many zeros,
it looked like a well-behaved bowl of Cheerios. Her husband
came into the dream with his boots on. *What do you got
there?* he wanted to know. She hated that her tongue had been
cut out. It was so frustrating. She tried to say *nothing*. She tried
to say *none of your business* but she ended up sounding
like a washing machine coming out of the spin cycle
and so he laughed. *What do you got there?* he said louder.
She surprised him by ripping up the lease of their marriage,
right in front of him, she just tore it in two. *Now, why do you go
and do that*, he wanted to know, but she was already busy
waking up.

The judge wanted to know if the daycare teacher
could remember anything about the girl's mother
and the teacher changed her voice into preschool
scissors and carefully cut around the words she was preparing
to say. When she pulled the words out, they remained
joined as well as individual silhouettes representing "tired"
and "not quite understanding the care the rough gem
of childhood required." What she said also resembled
a janitor's bucket and mop and everyone on the jury
admired how she sloshed gamely into her testimony,
how, at first, it seemed she was just spreading the same
dirty water around, but when she was done the floor
indeed looked cleaner to them. They didn't like hearing
that the parents hadn't cried when collecting the girl's
sweater or her Sailor Moon lunch box. Her Sailor Moon
lunch box was enough to send four of the ladies on the jury
scurrying into their purses for something, anything
to relieve the wicks in their lanterns from being
blown out.

The mother had held the girl's bear up to her
chest and it reported that the girl's heart was a bowl
of oatmeal that may be a little too hot to eat
but would soon cool and be just right. The doctor
had agreed on this assessment and showed the court
her notes. The mother had also held the girl's bear
to the girl's wrist and the bear reported that though
the girl's pulse was sort of hibernating, it would soon
wake and be ferociously hungry. Again, the doctor
subdued her alligator bag and removed her notes
from its teeth. The jury nodded but the lawyer
wanted to know why the doctor hadn't held the bear
up to the child's chest herself. Her office, she explained,
didn't come equipped with a bear to do the examination
properly so she relied on the mother to hold up the bear.
Order, the judge yelled, pounding his wife's headache
onto his agenda and everyone looked a little tarnished
but put their shoes back on. The lawyer asked for a recess
to do a little research on the very weighty subject
of bears and was granted ten minutes.

The lawyer asked the doctor about her relationship
to bears. Did she, for example, trust them? It depended,
she said, looking at the jury, if the bear was male
or female. The lawyer asked what that had to do with
anything and the doctor took this opportunity to explain
the variations of hunger to the court. The girl's ghost
had let itself in and had taken off its rain boots, putting
them up against the wall which was an old, old habit.
The ghost also hung up its raincoat and then sat down
with its hands folded and waited. The daycare teacher
wondered who was wearing perfume and looked around,
the ghost waved at the teacher who, sadly, didn't wave back
having closed her eyes to taste the delicious smell
a little better. The doctor had to agree that yes, a stethoscope
would have given a more accurate reading of the girl's heart rate
and pulse but the mother couldn't afford a stethoscope. The bear,
as she understood, had been given to the girl by a relative
when the girl was born. Objection, another lawyer insisted,
and the girl's father lit a small fire in his crotch and wished
there were more windows in the courtroom.

The doctor explained how she didn't like to
get her hands sticky and so would often not
examine her young patients, relying instead
on the wireless connection she felt between
herself and the patients' parents. Had she realized,
the lawyer wanted to know, that she had increased
the child's dosage thirteen times in the year she treated
her and that the child had not yet grown all of her teeth.
Not having grown all of her teeth wasn't a problem
on the kind of medication the child was on, the doctor
explained. She had been prescribed antipsychotic
medication for the very reason of not having all
of her teeth. And the fact that she was still in diapers
necessitated the second drug for the mental rash
children who are bipolar often develop. The lawyer
asked the doctor if there was a part of the brain
where this rash would appear and the doctor said yes,
a very specific part of the brain but, unfortunately,
she didn't have her address book with her and didn't know
how to best contact it. The girl's father, at this point, was throwing
photos on the fire of his crotch and the girl's mother, at the other end
of the table, was holding her glass of water so tight,
her knuckles were thirsty.

The girl's ghost was not necessarily a ghost
but more a representative of the girl's curiosity.
She moved with an ease that belied her death
and sat between her parents. The fire on her father's
crotch immediately went out and her mother's hold
on her water glass lightened. The girl wanted her bear.
She wanted to hold the bear to her heart and hear
for herself. Why would she believe anything
they told her? She could trust the bear. The times it insisted
she was in a forest and would soon come to its edge.
She didn't understand why her mouth was filled
with sand and kept emptying it like a shoe.
She couldn't taste the window she put her tongue to
so tried licking it like a popsicle. It wasn't that she missed
her mother and father, she just liked the cooking smell
of their clothes and thought she was hungry. Her daycare
teacher kept trying to hand her flowers but when she
reached out to take them, her teacher busied herself
with the Kleenex they'd turn into and wouldn't look up.

The father rubbed two teenage girls together and started
another fire. He wasn't on trial here and they couldn't
prove that he hadn't cried when his daughter died.
He opened a beer and drank it in silence. He had hoisted
his living room chair into the court. No one
even noticed when he took a piss. That was just like them,
he thought, filthy rich with buttons. He spit
into the gutter and thought about the city bus.
How the occasional arm would reach up to ring
the bell for an approaching stop and how, sometimes,
that arm was young. His wife was a burned sausage
and a hard boiled egg, only fatter. He had married her
in high school to get out of math. There used to be a room
in his thinking that had a lamp and some bookshelves.
He'd sit in there and take a thought down, read it
to the end. When he started taking fly swatters
for his anxiety, he couldn't find the door. When he complained
to the doctor that he couldn't find the door, the doctor prescribed
him a key ring he attached to his belt. Occasionally, he'd
find a key at work and clip it on. The keys would chime together
and he'd think about bare arms. He didn't tell the doctor
how he started self-medicating with shower curtains
and ankle socks.

The lawyer wanted to know how many children
she sees in a day and the doctor asked to see
his watch. Because he suffers from attention deficit
disorder, time is an issue for him, she explained.
She sees a child every twenty minutes but sometimes
twenty minutes to a person suffering like him feels like waiting
in line to renew his driver's license and other times,
twenty minutes feels like plenty of time to drive
the three hours it takes to get there. Did he understand
what she means? she wanted to know. Order, the judge
called, hammering his own watch, springing his day
into unordered hours to make room for at least a martini
and a minute of quiet when he finally did get home.
She can see up to three children an hour,
she explained carefully and she had won the speed writing
competition in her graduating class which means
that each of these children can take, on the average,
as many shovels as she can prescribe. This twenty
minutes, the lawyer wanted to know, did it involve
surgery?

The ghost of the girl hoisted the shovel to show
the jury what had been prescribed to her. She tried
telling them that all she could do with this shovel
was to dig holes she kept falling into. One of the jurors
was watching her so she showed how she had to stand on
a chair to manoeuvre the shovel to actually dig
a hole. The carpet in the court room wouldn't
cooperate, however, and so the ghost got frustrated
and kicked the shovel, which would often happen at home.
Her mother would then pull her off the chair
and put her in the bathtub without any water.
This made swimming and fishing extremely difficult,
she tried explaining to the juror. All she ever wanted
to do was to float in the bath. Sometimes her mother
would forget that she had locked her in there until
the mother had to pee. Then it would be funny
and her father would laugh and laugh until fires started
in his ears which would make him mad.

The lawyer wanted to slow things down and hear more
about his condition so the doctor prescribed him a chair
and prescribed the jury some crackers and cheese.
The doctor made herself comfortable and hung her diplomas
in the witness stand. An hour to someone with your disorder,
she explained, requires a backhoe and an apology.
The lawyer loosened his tie and put up his feet. The girl's mother
felt herself leaving her body. She could only hope, at this point,
to land in a room that was welcoming and didn't have any sharp
implements or her father. And at first, she didn't know where
she was, just that there were flowers and benches.
Her daughter was floating in the fountain and her other kids
were weaving leaves into her hair. She helped them pick flowers
that matched the girl's dress and showed them how they could
use the buttonholes to anchor the blossoms. She decided to carry
her daughter to one of the benches and was surprised
by the weight of her. There was no one around now,
her children off to find a flower that was more orange
than what was growing around the fountain. For the moment,
she had the girl to herself. The girl, who was learning
to sing at school because of her songbird. She had never
been given a bird when she was a girl and so when
she tried singing now, she was dismayed by the gravel
in her mouth and how the trees smirked and pointed.

The juror who had taken the sunflower seed to turn the thermostat
of her own childhood down was panicked that no one else saw
the sturdy flame of the girl's father's crotch. She looked to the judge
but he was trying to pour water without getting any ice
and the daycare teacher was busy braiding her dismay
to make an indoor/outdoor mat that someone else could use.
The lawyer asked the doctor about how the mother managed
to up her daughter's dosage without the doctor's consent.
The doctor explained that, as she said, she relies on binoculars,
mirrors, bears or whatever kind of wireless system there is
between the parents of her patients that can keep her informed
of their medical condition. Often in these cases, when the children
are too young to articulate how they're feeling,
their parents karaoke how their children's diagnosis
is progressing. In this case, the child's mother told her that the child
was driving her crazy. That she wouldn't put away her toys
and would often try to push her parents out of the way
when they insisted she do something she didn't want to.
The medication she prescribed is often used as an internal
way to chide the child to better behave. There are many
numbers, the doctor concluded, to back her up.

Poverty had ruined the girl's mother's skin.
Her family's particular poverty travelled in a cluster
huddled like old women. It would breathe on the milk in the fridge
and curdle it. It was more a poverty of spirit. The chair
in the living room, for example, couldn't hold a cushion.
No matter how many times the mother would plump
the chair up, sitting in it was as uncomfortable as being cross-
examined. Poverty would file away at the father's voice
until his words grew teethy at the edges. It would sometimes
steal his words and hide them in the basement until
the sound of them furred with mould. No one noticed
when poverty arrived in the courtroom except the ghost
of the girl. She stuck out her tongue and pulled her ears
but it wasn't interested in laughing. It placed its hands
on as many coffee cups as it could before it was told
to sit down. It was a kind of game and poverty kept score
by counting the number of people who exclaimed how fast
their coffee had gone cold.

The doctor on the stand explained that being loud
and silly were often prevalent signs of a bipolar child.
The lawyer wondered if the doctor could give an example.
The girl often thought she was a truck, the doctor offered,
and the jury nodded, checking off both loud and silly
in their notes. And the loud part? the lawyer asked.
Her motor, the doctor explained. Objection, one of the lawyers
complained and the lawyers conferred with the judge
about the qualitative nature of motors. The ghost of the girl
remembered being a truck and put her key in the ignition,
but poverty snickered at how it had siphoned
her gas. The doctor explained that one of the pills
was like a truck stop in layman's terms. It offered the girl a place
to take a quick nap and eat a sandwich on the side
of the highway she was travelling. The ghost of the girl
wanted to tell the doctor that she hadn't been driving
on a highway but had steered herself down the hallway
back into her room that she shared with her sister
because she was going to make breakfast for the ants
climbing into her window. The mother turned and looked
at her and the ghost of the girl swallowed a pill shaped
like the girl and sat under the chair she'd been standing on.

The doctor told the lawyer the girl had also been
very reckless. Could you give an example? the lawyer
asked, and the doctor recounted a visit where the girl
was a caterpillar one minute and then a witch the next.
Poverty could have told the courtroom the girl
had been a butterfly until it had plucked off her wings
but it was saving its voice for the opera, it scoffed
to itself. One of the jury members had a grandson
who thought he was a dog and her daughter-in-law
put a bowl on the floor so he could eat from it.
What's the name of the medication the girl was given
for being a caterpillar, she whispered to her neighbour juror,
and, referring to his notes to get it right, offered C–l–o–n–i
before poverty gobbled the rest of the tablets from the man's mouth.
The lawyer reminded the jury that the girl had been
a caterpillar and THEN a witch all in the twenty minutes
his client had seen the girl for her appointment. That's pretty
reckless in his books, he confided, which they all wrote down.

Sleeplessness was another symptom, the doctor explained
and the lawyer wanted to know if one had to be two-
and-a-half to be diagnosed with bipolar or could anyone
have it? Anyone, the doctor announced looking widely
around the room. Poverty tried eating her look but choked
on the saw blade of her aura and coughed the look
back up like steel wool. The girl often woke in the night, the doctor
explained to the jury, and the mother was at her wit's end.
The father laughed at the idea of the mother's wit
and the jury noted his laugh. It smoked like a cigar
and leered like a pervert, one of the jurors would report later
and the rest of the jury agreed, he laughed like a pervert
all right. Don't all two-year-olds wake up in the night? the lawyer
asked. In this particular case, the doctor noted, given the
caterpillar and witch recklessness, the loud motor and the silliness
of a girl being a truck, the girl's sleeplessness indicated
that the synapses in her brain were not releasing enough serotonin
which is generally where lullabies incubate. The drug the girl
was given would increase lullabies while inhibiting or closing
the window after they'd been released so they couldn't get back in.
So the drug was also an inhibitor, the lawyer said, grasping,
and poverty swooped in and ate his tie dissuading the idea
that he had formally dressed for the occasion. Objection,
one of the lawyers yelled, and poverty was told if it didn't
sit down it would have to leave the courtroom.

Hyperactivity, the lawyer said. Tell us a little about that.
The doctor cleared her throat of her siblings and all
their trophies. Poverty had to hold itself back when it saw
the trophies glinting like treasure. The ghost of the girl
sat on the daycare teacher's lap and the teacher
told her a story about a red hen who couldn't find
her mixing bowl to make her bread. The ghost
of the girl nuzzled between the teacher's breasts.
She felt sad for the red hen because she, as a girl, had always
lost things. She was told she'd lose her head
if it wasn't screwed on so tight. Which is why she'd wake
in the middle of the night, her heart alarming: Wake up! Do
something! Don't forget to screw your head on! The doctor
was explaining how in a hyperactive child, the child
couldn't finish a sentence and would follow every shiny
thing they could find. The girl, for example, would ask
her mother for her keys, find something to play with
on the doctor's desk and forget about the keys entirely,
all the while being a caterpillar then a witch. Would the caterpillar
or the witch ask for the keys? the lawyer wanted to know.
That depended on the girl's mood, the doctor explained.
The girl was also extremely moody.

Poverty was taunting the girl's father's fire. Did he want
a training bra, poverty asked and the father sizzled
in his seat. Order, the judge yelled. Did he want
some panties? The father slumped and the fire
in his crotch flared. Order, the judge yelled and the father
sat up, trying to hide the fire from the judge who had already
warned him about open flames in his courtroom. Poverty
gobbled up the father's shame for its salt. The lawyer
asked the doctor if the girl had exhibited other behaviour
that warranted increasing her dosage from a single pill
to an entire orchestra complete with the several trumpets
she had been given to drown out her own loudness.
She suffered anxiety, the doctor told the jury, as well as rage
and low self-esteem. Objection, the courtroom yelled,
to which the lawyers objected and the judge pounded
on the doctor's prescription pad for order and then called
a recess so he could take a piss and look out at the parking
lot from his office. Often, he'd been described as being
a little Zen.

The jury went to their room to stretch their legs.
One of the jurors wanted to know if anyone else
had seen the doctor clear her throat of her siblings
and their trophies, but the rest of them had been watching
the father tend his fire. They agreed that he was a guy
who needed professional help. No wonder the girl couldn't sleep,
one of the jurors said, her father was literally on fire. That
had to bother her, they agreed. And the fire is in his crotch,
another juror exclaimed, and he's feeding it with young girls
dressed to play tennis. And those short shorts, a juror
whistled, that guy needs a hobby. One of the jurors cleared
her throat of her grandmother's crochet hook and offered
that she once thought she was a turtle. They all looked at her.
A turtle? That's nothing, another juror added, he used to think
he was a backhoe. A backhoe? Because the door was closed,
poverty couldn't come in and turn off the faucet. One of them
thought that they were reincarnated and used to be a saint.
One of them wished he could have been blue, he thought blue
was the best colour when he was a kid. Another thought the donkey
on his father's farm could understand him when he talked.
The juror recounted how the donkey's eyes were a cross
between Jesus and Santa and the donkey forgave him
for everything including stealing his sister's money the time
she lost her tooth.

The doctor examined her childhood in the mirror.
Her siblings were vacationing in her eyes and so she was
seeing them everywhere. She quickly uncapped a vial
and swallowed a moment when she had guessed
the word her father had been looking for. She swallowed
the spoon she had used to feed her mother after
the surgery then straightened her blazer and added a couple
of inches to her height. The ghost of the girl had been
taunting her all morning. Slithering under chairs
and then pointing her wand and casting a spell
so she'd turn into a peach. A peach. The doctor scoffed
at the idea of turning into a peach. It showed how little
any of these people really knew her. She'd never allow
herself to become a peach. She left the bathroom
to poverty greedily smucking up even the thought
of the fruit.

The father was having a talk to the fire. He'd allow
it to burn but only as embers. The fire snarled
at the idea of an elbow and the word *don't*. The father
shook his head and took a long drink from his beer.
That wouldn't do, he'd have to sizzle the fire but he didn't
want to waste good beer on it. The fire jeered. Pussy,
it called the father, and momentarily the father fell into
its flames before pulling himself back out. His daughter
was dead, he reminded himself and unplugged the security
camera. His daughter was dead. He found his wife
and unscrewed her fuse so her eyes went out. He found the bathroom
and pissed in the garbage. Fuckers, he said to the mirror
and the mirror scoffed back. Fuckers, it said which alerted
the father to a fighting stance. Listen, motherfuck, he said
to it. Listen motherfuck, it said back to him so he slammed
his beer into its mouth and the thing broke just like that.
He didn't have anything to do with it.

The lawyer referred to his notes after retying his tie.
He had written down "Florida" and "time-share". He had written
down "Mensa", meaning him. The doctor was someone
he could have dated if he was ten years older. He had caught
her looking at him and had made her blush. A sweet rosé
with a fruity aftertaste, he ascertained. He cleared his throat
of the snow he'd been in charge of clearing all his life.
All his goddamned life. Anxiety, he heard himself say. Tell me
about the girl's anxiety. Yeah, the fire burning in the father's
crotch said, give us a camp song about worry, which made the father
hunch over himself as if praying. The girl was extremely
anxious, the doctor said. About what? the lawyer wanted
to know. The girl's mother had been stirring the pot of how
things happened until it thickened and had hypnotized herself
into believing the whole thing was a kind of pudding they'd all
be able to eat after dinner. Dinner, poverty slurped, pushing its
sleeves up and getting ready. The girl was especially anxious
around bedtime, the doctor disclosed.

The ghost of the girl remembered her feet and practised
making footsteps. She put one foot down and then the other
and then tried finding the step she had just taken but had lost
it. The doctor was talking like a boss about bedtime but the ghost
of the girl held the girl like her bear and told her that it was okay,
she had so many lullabies they spilled out of her like a kind of
night light. Even her mother's hands that were shark fins, circling
the girl's body, stitching the blankets so she was sewn
to the bed didn't scare her. The girl was a caterpillar but a beautiful
caterpillar who was searching for her wings that had been eaten
by the truck that filled their hearts with oil. She was walking outside
at night and had lost her wings because she had forgotten to wake up
in time to wind them tighter, but now she had a wand
and could change bedtime into morning and everyone had to
get up. And she could change the doctor into a bottle opener
and her father would use her to open his beers and the doctor's mouth
would be open like this: O.

The mother missed her tongue. She'd often taste things
she hadn't said for years and longed for the love she once
licked like a stamp. Often in dreams, she'd use it to properly smell
a flower or to taste the door of her grandmother's house.
The doctor used her tongue like a putty knife. She smoothed the
drywall of her talk until you couldn't even see the holes
that had been there. The girl's mother used to ask the doctor
if it was normal for a child to want to hang on the way the girl
hung on. It depends, the doctor had told her, on what
the girl thinks she is holding on to. If the mother was a piece
of wood, for example, and the girl believed she was drowning,
then it would make sense that the girl would want to hang
on to her. But if it was the mother who was drowning
and the girl was hanging on to her like a weight or a curse,
then that was something they could medicate. Either way,
she'd prescribe the girl a lifeboat, if the mother wanted her to.

The lawyer wanted to know more about the girl's
rage. She would growl, the doctor confessed. Objection,
one of the lawyers yelled. She would growl when she believed
she was a bear, the doctor conceded. How often did she
believe she was a bear, the lawyer prodded. The frequency
that the girl believed she was a bear was alarming,
the doctor confessed. The mother would use her bathroom mirror
to contact the doctor and the doctor would respond
with her prescription pad. They'd often discuss the girl,
who was kept in her room when she exhibited bear-like
behaviour. Such as? the lawyer excavated. Such as growling
and waving her arms in the air as if they were paws.
Did she acknowledge any relation to the bear that was held
to her heart? the lawyer wanted to know. She said that bear,
the bear held to her heart was her mother, the doctor whispered
and two of the jurors had to leave the courtroom to catch
their breath, which poverty had feasted on without being noticed.

The judge was beginning to see where all of this
was going. He had listened to the doctor explain
the various symptoms the girl had exhibited
and had understood that the doctor often needed to pull over
in her talk to confer with her map. The mother
had her back to his bench and was busy stirring up her version,
testing it for sweetness. And the father, the father
was nothing but a hard-on. And if poverty ate any more
chairs he'd have to shut this whole thing down
until they could find some more. He had considered
asking the ghost of the girl to leave the proceedings
but no one else could see her and he had to admit she had him
bedazzled. He trusted the daycare teacher the most
because she had counted out the cookies and made sure
each of them had their fair share. She also looked him
in the eye when she told him how proud she was
of how he was handling all of this. As a father, she meant.

The low self-esteem often presented itself the most clearly
when the girl was playing house, the doctor told the jury.
One afternoon when they were using coffee cups to communicate,
the mother had told her the girl's sister was pretending
to be a mother but the girl didn't want to be the girl,
she wanted to be the house. You mean with a driveway
and a front door? the lawyer asked. Exactly, the doctor confirmed,
with a kitchen and a hallway. And a bedroom? the lawyer
induced rapidly. That is why she prescribed the welcome mat
and the chimney. Often, bipolar children need more keys for the doors
between the cells in their brains. You see, the doctor said to the jury,
the cells lock certain brain chemicals out and the child's happiness
wouldn't feel welcome. Has this been proven in clinical trials?
the lawyer asked. There have been clinical trials, the doctor
confirmed. And so the medication she added to her lunch box
was shaped like a unicorn but at its heart had hardware
that could unlock the front doors of the cells in her brain
and allow her sense of safety and confidence in. And just exactly
how many unicorns was this girl taking a day? the lawyer
wanted to know. That is difficult to say, given the mythical
quality of the creature, the doctor replied, and how hard it is
to actually see it. Objection, one of the lawyers yelled.

Poverty didn't know the first thing about eating
a unicorn. It gnawed at its horn but the glitter
settled in poverty's cavities which caused pain
to spark in its ears. It picked up a leg
but the delicious smell of green dazed it and poverty
found itself sitting down, scraping green out of the unicorn's
hoof. The ghost of the girl showed it how to start
a plant by placing the green at the bottom of a glass of water.
The plant quickly took root and offered its leaves
which poverty ate immediately. It was surprising how nourished
poverty felt after eating those leaves. The ghost of the girl
put her hand on the unicorn and the unicorn told her
that unicorns had never been captured in pill form.
What the girl had been prescribed was actually an elk
and even then not a real elk but a synthetic version
that probably made her feel worse. Poverty didn't have a belt
to undo, it was feeling that plenished.

The lawyer wanted to know if the girl had shown
any improvement after the dosage of unicorn
had been increased and the doctor admitted not at first.
Her mother reported that the girl often responded
with siren sounds when asked anything. Siren as in
fire truck? the lawyer asked. Siren as in ambulance,
the doctor made clear. In the last few months of her life,
she responded as if everything was an emergency, the doctor
elaborated, which made life very difficult for the mother,
who at that point also needed several plungers prescribed.
Where was the girl's father during this time? the lawyer asked.
The girl's father had overdosed on undergarments
and had become a liability to the family, which is why
she changed his prescription from trench coats to bricks and nuns.
As in all such cases, it's very difficult if the patient
refuses to take his medication, the doctor told the jury,
and the father, at this point, was not only not taking the medication
prescribed but was also taking illegal drugs like lip gloss
and hair accessories.

The mother remembered the sirens and wished
she had her wallet with her. She was medicating herself
with small change, as hard as it was to swallow.
The daycare teacher had reined the unicorn away
from poverty and left it grazing on the bald heads
of the courtroom press gallery, which was inspiring
many of the reporters to consider novel and poetry writing,
making concentration difficult. The mother cleared her tongue
from her throat and everyone turned to look at her.
She could feel them all like torches
and her polyester pants sweat close to igniting.
Poverty came and stood near her because it had known
her the longest and could still taste her tongue. The jury
wondered if now would be a good time to take a break.
Not yet, the judge ruled. The doctor still had to explain
medical testing.

Medical testing for bipolar in a two-year-old
involves testing the child's ability to enunciate
words as well as measuring the level of concentration
the child can apply to a task at hand. But the testing?
the lawyer coaxed. The testing involves examining how the cells
in the child's brain are communicating. And the brain? the lawyer asked.
Is in the child's head, the doctor confirmed. The girl exhibited
an abnormal amount of rage, the doctor continued,
and would often refuse to listen to her mother. Is there a blood test
that can be done to confirm the diagnosis? This girl
did have blood, the doctor confirmed. And her brain
was in her head, the lawyer reiterated. Yes, the doctor
said. Aggressive behaviour is common when looking for
symptoms. Because the girl was bipolar? the lawyer prompted.
Yes, exactly, the doctor cemented. The father had taken the rifle
from his childhood and was cleaning it on the table. He had also cleared
his throat of all its hands and they were now walking on their own accord,
groping. The ghost of the girl stood on a chair and roared.

The girl's bear heard the ghost of the girl's roar. The bear
had been sleeping. Normally, the sunlight would guide
the bear from her cave and she would then amble through
the woods until she came to the crumbling edge where the girl
lived, but there was no light to guide the bear now.
She pawed at the dark but couldn't find an opening and so bellowed
back to the ghost of the girl a message that the bear
would soon be there. The ghost of the girl standing on the chair
snarled back to the bear that the father had his rifle out
and the bear was safer in its cave. The bear missed the girl's heart,
the bear told the ghost of the girl, but so did the ghost of the girl.
What was it like? the ghost of the girl asked, and the bear
said it was like silver fish in a river, each beat sure and strong
and swimming with the current. How did the bear find the girl?
the ghost of the girl wanted to know. By smell, by the honey smell
of the girl the bear had found the girl lying there that last time,
on the floor without her heart.

The lawyer wanted to get the symptoms straight.
The girl suffered from anxiety, rage, recklessness
and low self-esteem? Yes, said the doctor. The girl was defiant
and wasn't sleeping? the lawyer queried. That is correct,
the doctor harmonized. And the girl could not pronounce
her words? Objection, one lawyer thought but did not say
because he was always saying it and was getting sick
of the sound of his own voice: she had only been two,
yadda, yadda, yadda. She was only this tall, whatever,
whatever, whatever. The part of the girl's brain affected by her bipolar
condition was the *amygdala*? the lawyer continued, walking over
the saying of this part of the brain as if it were ice and he was wearing
the wrong shoes. Correct, the doctor approved. And because
you don't have your address book, you cannot tell us exactly
where the *amygdala* is? That is also correct, the doctor
said, she had no way to get in contact with that part
of the brain without her address book. A doctor has to remember
a great many things, she offered, and she could barely remember
how to make her favourite and very simple balsamic vinegar
salad dressing without looking it up online. She turned to the jury
and waited until they laughed before pushing her hair behind
her smile and adjusting her breast size.

The girl had begun crying over very small things
by the time she was prescribed the rocking chairs
and the tether, the doctor told the court. How small
are we talking about, the lawyer wanted to know,
small as the head of a pin or really microscopic?
Yes, the doctor confirmed emphatically. The girl could smell
germs on her father and refused to sit on his knee.
She was also convinced the ants her mother killed
were screaming and crying when they were being triaged
by the paramedic ants. The lawyer conferred with his notes.
You and the girl's mother met in the Save Easy parking lot
and discussed the thorns the girl was experiencing
and thought an increase in herbicide would be the way
to get rid of the bramble the girl was speaking. You spoke
about increasing the herbicide because the girl had developed
a severe case of knotweed and the mother was concerned
the girl was driving her crazy and that she was at her wit's
end. The girl was driving her crazy, the lawyer repeated
with the subwoofer of implication in his voice and the speed of fate
in his delivery. And she was at her wit's end, he reiterated
slowly for the benefit of the courtroom. Poverty ate the meringue
of his performance with glee. Wit's end tasted the best,
it agreed.

The mother had stacked the cans the coupons had bought
against winter. In this way, she was an excellent warrior.
She had enough stewed tomatoes to hide the taste of
anything. She was trying to figure out her best defence
against this courtroom. She was wearing her fanciest stretch
and it was purple. She had washed her hair in the sink
and put up a fight with her chair. It was too small, she had snarled
but it was stubborn and just sat there. She wiggled her ass
into it argumentatively adding the weight of her childhood
for good measure. It creaked but didn't budge.
She pulled herself closer to the table and used her elbows
as leverage to plant herself heavier into the chair
but the chair and table, she quickly realized, were in cahoots
and so her plan didn't work. The chair, she concluded,
had to be bipolar and so she tried to get the doctor's attention
by tapping her tennis shoe. The doctor was wearing open toe
sandals and everyone in the courtroom seemed enthralled
by her toes. The mother risked writing the doctor a note
but got stuck on what exactly to say.

So the girl had been prescribed herbicide and unicorns
as well as a rocking chair and a tether all in the short time
of her nap? The doctor scoffed, briefly, and corrected the lawyer.
This child, she reminded the courtroom, never took a nap.
Okay, the lawyer said, scratching his head with his pencil,
but the girl must have fallen asleep otherwise how could she wet
her bed? The girl would fall asleep only to wet the bed, the doctor
concurred. She either fell asleep to wet the bed or to wake up
screaming, the doctor explained patiently. Bipolar children
rarely need sleep because they can refuel by recharging themselves
with everyone else's energy, the doctor elaborated. The mother,
at this point, had been depleted. This is why the doctor prescribed
the mother a farmer and two acres of land so someone else
could plow, she explained. The lawyer nodded and looked at
the jury. We all know what it feels like to need someone else
to do the plowing, don't we? he reasoned with them. Poverty
had eaten the judge's gavel so he couldn't demand order
when the farmers in the crowd objected to the amount
of plowing they were doing when already so much of their day
was genetically modified. The judge had to use his shoe
and then his briefcase and finally the cricket sound option
on his cellphone to establish order. The sound of the crickets
brought a pond into the courtroom and a whiff of vacation.
Even the prosecuting lawyer had to admit he felt
a little rested and serene at the thought of the month
of July rolled out into bulrushes under a testimony of clouds
that had witnessed summer.

Poverty ate the barbequed idea of summer with a heap
of onions and mustard. It slurped at the lemonade
puddled in the pause in the courtroom. The girl's father
felt the metallic hook of a bikini pierce his lip so he bit
into it. Briefly, he imagined the long waist and belly button
ring where his hand was moving but then felt the jerk
of the hook tear into his lip and heard the rusted laugh
of poverty watching him squirm. It threw him a rind
of swimming pool, the peel of tank top but he couldn't breathe
in all the young tits at once and the hands
he had coughed up held him under water.
The ghost of the girl watched him. She understood the crickets
had been mechanical. Real crickets would never let themselves
be caught in a phone. She had met several crickets
in the marsh between the floor and the fog she found herself in.
They were royalty but insisted on bowing to her.
Her appearance had startled them but they quickly
remembered protocol and bowed again and offered her
the choicest place to sit, where the view
went on forever and the shade was particularly sweet.

The lawyer read the statement from the daycare's nurse
to the courtroom: the girl had been too floppy. Too floppy,
he bellowed, to sit in a chair. He looked at the doctor. Does this
ring a bell? he asked. Yes, the doctor replied. It is common
for the transformation between oppositional to a more normalized
and adjusted behaviour to appear as a sort of floppiness, she confirmed.
Is that the medical term for that transition? he asked. Yes,
floppiness, she said gravely. Thank you, the lawyer
curtsied and the doctor nodded with the accomplishment
of playing such a difficult musical piece properly. The girl had been
too floppy to walk up the stairs or be the cow
in the Farmer in the Dell BECAUSE she was beginning to make
the transition to being a better behaved citizen, the lawyer
said to the courtroom. Ordinarily, the girl refused to be the rooster
and would demand snack time immediately upon arrival
because of her insatiable hunger but her inability to actually climb
the stairs or take off her coat indicates that she was beginning
to acquiesce to the role of whatever farm animal she was being
requested to represent. He turned to the doctor, this is a huge
and positive development, am I right, doctor? Yes, she said,
huge. Poverty ate the word huge like it was candy and had to agree,
it was huge all right.

The daycare teacher held a chick in her hand.
It peeped and looked at her quizzically. She cupped
her palm a little closer to it and it nestled into
her hand as if it belonged there. The ghost
of the girl was watching and felt the pan where her heart
used to bake heat up without the usual feeling of expansion.
She stood as close as she could to the daycare teacher.
The daycare teacher was cooing to the chick
and the chick was a soft down of happiness. It spurred
its fluff so that the ghost of the girl could hear it
purr. The chick's eyes deepened so the ghost of the girl
could look into them like sunglasses, the chick's heart
right there in front of her not just beating but feathered
with a kind of love and well-being. The ghost of the girl
wrestled poverty under the table, holding its throat
with a strength that surprised her. Don't, she said
with teeth she didn't even know she had. Don't,
and poverty slithered away broken and torn. It would snap
that chick in two, it promised her. It would chew
it up like a marshmallow. She growled and poverty
paled like an Aspirin, sneering at her. Boo, it said.

The girl's mother was at her wit's end
with the pattern of the floor in the courtroom.
It wasn't just the diamond pattern repeated over and over
like marriage proposals that was driving her crazy (no,
no and no). It was the way it didn't collect money
or anything useful, just bits of cat hair from the jurors' pets
and the hairnet of coughs the judge and lawyers kept flinging.
She could tell the way the flooring cut in under the radiators
that it had been laid by an amateur. Everyone knows
that the cut has to be angled. And the girl hadn't been
floppy but easier to dress. The girl's mother
looked at the girl's father who had gotten himself into trouble
again. There he was trying to stuff himself back
in before anyone saw his eighteen-wheeler, his smoker's
hack. She gargled his name every morning
before spitting it out. Marriage. She had told him
not to get caught. She told him there was no ghost
at the kitchen table but he kept freaking the fuck out,
locking them up and then throwing away the key. Because
he had laughed and poverty agreed, picking its teeth
and then eating the plate.

Can you tell me what happened the morning of January 16th?
the lawyer asked the doctor. The drapes were drawn in his voice
and the courtroom darkened. The ghost of the girl felt the flashlights
where her eyes had been narrow. She could barely see herself
in his talk. The girl's mother had shouted for the doctor
very early in the morning, the doctor told the lawyer.
Very early, the lawyer repeated. How early, was the moon still
in the sky? The doctor assumed so, she slept with a mask, she told him,
and had to be in denial of anything as big as the sky in order to get
to sleep. Did she contact the mother right away? the lawyer persisted.
No, the doctor confessed, and the jury leaned forward to hear
the nuance crouched in her reason. She had appointments
with other children who were standing on furniture
and throwing things and she had to make sure they were being given
medication. She normally made contact with parents in the late afternoon,
she concluded, when there was less chance they'd be at home.
Pardon? the lawyer said. When there was less chance that she'd
be disturbed, the doctor edited. The jury nodded, okay, they thought,
that made more sense. How did she contact the girl's mother
at that time of day? the lawyer asked. First she tried by pigeon
but didn't get a reply so she switched to cloud; again, no reply.
She then used her stir stick then her lipstick and then her nail file.
Still no reply? the lawyer clarified. The doctor nodded no.
Then what? the lawyer prompted. The doctor looked up from
her hands in her lap and made eye contact with the jury,
then she used the phone. The what? the lawyer asked. Objection,
another lawyer yelled. Order, the judge demanded, and poverty
feasted on everyone's surprise like buttered popcorn.

The girl's mother had her hand on her ear. The doctor's voice
refused to leave the nest it had made there. Are you sure?
it kept chirping and the thud of *yes* made the girl's mother
curl her hand into the fist that pounded the voice quiet,
feathers everywhere. Poverty had collected the feathers
into a pot and dumped a can of stewed tomatoes onto them.
You have to eat, it insisted, even in your state. And it guided
a spoon to the girl's mother's mouth. Yum, it said and the girl's
mother swallowed the doctor's *Are you sure?* until it settled
in her stomach like a baked potato or a rock. Or until she was
sure. Did she need anything, the doctor had asked and without
waiting for a reply prescribed her salt for her driveway
and a tea cozy for her heart. She instructed the girl's mother
to tie herself to her version of events with a nylon rope and to knot
it twice. Do not increase the dosage of the rope, the doctor
warned. She told the mother not to talk to reporters even if they deep
fried their microphones or promised her a cruise. A cruise,
the mother had said weakly. It won't be a real cruise, the doctor
had whispered, just a picture of a cruise ship from one of those
travel magazines that were free in the mall. Oh, the girl's
mother said, not able to understand anything after
she said she was sure.

How many unicorns were found in the girl's bloodstream?
the lawyer asked. The doctor checked her cellphone
before replying that there had been three times the maximum
dosage of fairy tales where unicorns were usually sighted.
Can you give that to the court in layman's terms? the lawyer
requested. Yes, the doctor replied. There were enough unicorns
in the girl's bloodstream to fill a football field with the kind
of hope that would reverse climate change. Whoa, the lawyer
said. Indeed, the doctor agreed. And did you prescribe all
of those unicorns? the lawyer asked. I absolutely did
not, the doctor emphasized. Okay, the lawyer said, where
did all the unicorns come from? The doctor shrugged. This is often
the nature of unicorns, no one is sure where they are
and how to capture them. They are a rare drug and she only
prescribed it when she absolutely needed to because of the difficulty
of dispensing them. How often would you say you prescribed
unicorns in your practice? the lawyer pressured. The doctor nodded,
understanding the direction he was taking. About 99%
of the time, she said, given how frequently she was seeing
children exhibit bipolar symptoms. So, the lawyer concluded,
given how many children are diagnosed bipolar, a rare
and mystical drug was now being used in a more widespread,
common manner. Exactly, the doctor confirmed. Objection,
a lawyer was about to yell but poverty stole the word from his mouth
and steamed it with some paper before icing the goo of it
onto the walls.

Besides death, do we know of any other side effects?
the lawyer said, pursuing his case. The frontal cortex
of the patient's brain may atrophy taking on the properties
of an actual unicorn, like its horn, the doctor offered.
And? the lawyer persisted. And the synapses where unicorns
graze become so verdant, the brain stops functioning
and relies on the unicorns to replenish the neuron fields
of the patient's summer. Is that safe? the lawyer asked cautiously.
The doctor shrugged, there had been no long-term trials done
at this point so she couldn't say. Though this drug has been approved,
the lawyer said. Again, hard to say, the doctor replied. As she said,
unicorns were mythological and mystically inclined. I see, the lawyer
nodded, turning to the jury. The doctor prescribed the girl
medication to stabilize her condition, he told them. She had to trust
the girl's mother to monitor the dosage because the mother
was the one with the girl's bear and knew how her daughter's
heart was managing. If the girl's father had indeed become
a chainsaw on the night of January 15th, the girl's mother
could have asked to have more trees prescribed for the safety
of her family, the lawyer concluded, instead of worrying about
the landlord and his adversity to clear-cutting.

The daycare teacher put the painting apron
on the ghost of the girl. She poured a fresh cup of water
and handed her a paintbrush. The ghost of the girl
discovered that she could coax out the shine on the dullest
part of the table with her brush. She could enliven
the blue of the empty chairs. Poverty watched her
but couldn't see anything it could actually take away from her
so was suspicious. The girl drew the bear on the table's
surface and added the long rays of a cheerful sun above
her head. The bear could feel the heat of the sun
in the dark cavern she was stuck in. She lifted her snout
and drew the direction of it in, raising herself on her
hind legs and stretching. The ghost of the girl retraced
the bear's outline so she wouldn't fade. She retraced
the sun and then, refreshing her brush in water,
she drew the girl smiling and in a new dress.
The bear stood her full height and growled, pulling
up the small things with roots in her way. Poverty blew
its nose and ate the Kleenex. The girl's father cocked
his gun and aimed at the ceiling, firing at the tin cans
that were guarding against winter, firing off on the pets
he had never been allowed. He heard a young girl
squeal every time his gun went off. You like that?
he asked her.

The jury was told that the girl had been found
on the floor beside her parents' bed. Her arms
were described as sparrows that had once been inquisitive.
They were reminded how sparrows ignore any thought
of danger to investigate things they find alluring.
Members of the jury knew this of sparrows.
Many of them had bird feeders in their yard
or suction cupped to the windows of their apartments.
They were told that the girl's head was bigger
than her body because she'd still been a fledgling.
Poverty was having a field day with all the talk
of fledglings. Little jelly beans; unexpected disasters.
The way a fledgling would lose its balance and fall over.
Perfect, poverty said, popping another one in its mouth
and crunching.

The jury had heard how the girl's father rasped his stubble
on the silk of the illegal drugs he'd been taking. The mother
had spread silence like lard the night before the girl had died.
The apartment smelled of the cartilage holding the marriage
together and the silence that was smeared on the walls, greased
into the furniture. The girl's father kept saying: Do something!
while poverty licked their apartment like a porn star. The girl's
mother wiped her hands on her own shirt. Her lawyer wanted the jury
to know that the girl's mother had wiped her hands on her own
shirt. The girl had been a fledgling, he said. The girl was crying out
and the mother was under the instruction of the girl's doctor
to increase the dosage if the girl started sounding like a whole
flock. Remember, at this point, the father had traded in his hands
for saw blades, the girl's mother's lawyer told them. Remember
that the girl's mother still had hands, they were greasy
so she really couldn't grasp anything, let alone truly get a grip.
The jury was shown a photograph of the girl's body,
the angular shoulder blades where her wings hadn't been properly
wound. The diaper seemed too loose. Her bear, they noticed
wasn't anywhere near to her heart.

The jury deliberated about the distance between the bear
and the girl's heart. The judge had counselled them
to sit in the green pasture of their own conscience and clear
their minds of everything but birdsong but they couldn't get
the bear out of their talk. If the mother had been instructed
to use the bear to monitor the girl's heart, why was it so far
from the girl? And why was the mother smoking
so much air freshener? The doctor had not actually administered
any medication to the girl and they gagged at the smell of the father's
privacy. And why couldn't they plow their minds free
of how poverty had eaten everything but the mother was the one
that was so fat? The ghost of the girl wandered in and picked up
a pen. They had spelled the girl's name wrong so she fixed it, adding
a heart and some flowers, a squirrel. She moved the idea of the girl
and her bear away from the edge of the table. No one ever thinks
of the edge being so close. Or the drop so sudden.

The lawyer consulted his notes and counted a circus
of drugs prescribed by his client. He rounded it down
to a sideshow and increased the height of the tent
by a few feet to make it feel like there was more room
for a positive outcome. Poverty was nearby grazing on the smell
of his aftershave. It was fruity and woodsy, it decided,
rubbing it on the girl's father and then licking it off.
The girl's father swatted at poverty like a horsefly.
Yum, it said at the thought of that. The daycare teacher
was tired. She had rolled back every one of the balls
ever rolled to her. She had blessed each sneeze
and exclaimed over each bouquet of crooked flowers
drawn for her. The judge had retreated into a meditative
trance in his office and was filling his body with breath.
All past and future noise stopped and he was balancing
on the pointed and welcoming summit of the present moment.
He wasn't at all surprised to hear the bear in the courtroom
though no one else seemed to know it was there.
The jury was almost done deliberating but it no longer
mattered what the outcome was, he thought, opening
his eyes and getting up. The proper way to receive
a bear was with a welcome and a promise that no harm
would come to it. This much he was willing to do.

The bear had the ghost of the girl
in her arms when the judge came out
of his quarters. They looked at each other.
The idea of justice hung between them
like flypaper. They ignored poverty
and the smacking sounds it was making, feasting
off the trap. The bear put her head close to the ghost
of the girl's mouth and listened. She tasted
what the ghost said and then risked the sting
of many bees to put her snout in the hive
of the courtroom. I claim this girl, she said.
The judge nodded. She's always been mine,
the bear said and, again, the judge nodded, bowing
slightly. She was given to me. The bear tasted the silence
that met these words. Its broth was clear but without the fortitude
of meat. Poverty snuck up behind the bear and tried raking
her shadow with its fork. Without exertion, the bear
made ribbon of its pelt, tossing it to the father who laughed.
Again. This laugh was a kissing cousin to the laugh
of the morning the girl had been found. It was as inappropriate
as a party hat. The bear pulled her lips back and showed
her teeth. Her growl was as low and effective as forced air heating.
The judge used paperwork to deal with the drafts.

When the mother and bear faced each other, the bear snouted
at the word *mother* like a carcass, spent and boned. The mother
tried protecting her wishbone with her high school yearbook.
She inhaled deeply and held in her fear until she was stoned enough
to see headlights. Someone was tapping on her eardrum
with a rack of antlers. She couldn't hear words for the voices.
The bear had pulled the last velour off the word *mother*
and the memory of the girl was fading and then broken.
Carla felt something shift. She couldn't name what she had lost
but it had been lambswool soft and now her bones were grinding together
before fusing stiff. Someone was speaking then lifting her arm
to guide her. She stood and allowed herself to be led.
She had lost her tongue, she wanted to tell them. Briefly, she was
outside, the sky an endless grocery list of clouds. A maple tree shimmered
more laughter as her head was being lowered, as she was being put
into the back of a van. Her mother was waiting for her
with photos of Carla as a girl. You see, I never understood
what you had found so funny. Delighting in every damn thing,
her mother told her. Her father cuffed her to a metal pole
and injected her with his pipe smoke. None of your sass,
he said. Carla leaned back and heard a girl say something to her
so she bent closer to hear. The girl was lying
on a blanket, dishevelled and thin. Isn't she pretty, momma,
she said holding up a bear. Momma? Carla tried saying, grieving
her tongue, who is this momma?

The bear carried the ghost of the girl tenderly
in her teeth and ran until walls and verdict were replaced
by trees. She stood the ghost of the girl by the river.
She kept slipping so the bear moved her to a sapling and leaned her
into it. She waited to see if the ghost would slip again
but she stayed upright, squinting at the sun. What is that?
she wanted to know. That's your sister, the bear told her gently.
I drew her wrong, the ghost dismayed. The bear shook her head,
you were close, she said, then concentrated on the task
she'd set out to do. She threw the first fish back.
Too slow, the bear explained. The sapling was carbonating
the story it was giving the ghost with tender leaves that rose
in the telling like bubbles, bursting their green into the place
where her ears would be if the ghost of the girl had ears.
The bear was patient having grown old in the winters she'd spent
with the girl and her reach was slow. The girl had often groomed
the bear and gave her words to speak, then would sing the bear
more words that were lozenges of honey the bear would gulp.
Between them, there wasn't a moment they weren't famished.

The bear knew the second before she caught it
that she'd found the right one. She readied herself
for the feel of it, how it might overwhelm her
but once she held the fish it was more
like a homecoming than anything. The bear reveled
in the pure movement of it, its clamour for life.
It felt like this, she told the ghost of the girl
before placing the fish in the pan where the girl's heart
had been. The fish enchanted them by swimming
in protest. The girl glided back into her voice
long enough to say *oh*. *Oh*. Love trusted the bear to pick the fish
from the pan then and return it to its river. It would be easy
and proper to say, at this point, that several seasons later,
the tree surprised the bear by flowering; its fruit a succulence
that chimed with her loss a new kind of nourishment.

ACKNOWLEDGEMENTS

Thanks to the Canada Council, Arts Nova Scotia and Access Copyright Foundation Research Grants for the opportunity and time to defy schedule and create in the manner that suits me best: roaming and being a little feral. ¶ Thanks to my family and friends, my students and cohorts: my karass. Thanks to the good people of Halifax and beyond the bridges.

This book was designed and typeset in Quadraat by Andrew Steeves and printed offset and bound under the direction of Gary Dunfield at Gaspereau Press Limited, Kentville, Nova Scotia.

7   6   5   4   3   2   1

Library and Archives Canada Cataloguing in Publication

Goyette, Sue, author
    The brief reincarnation of a girl / Sue Goyette.

Poems.
ISBN 978-1-55447-146-1 (pbk.)

    I. Title.

PS8563.O934B75 2015   C811'.54   C2015-900713-5

GASPEREAU PRESS LIMITED ⁊ GARY DUNFIELD
& ANDREW STEEVES ⁊ PRINTERS & PUBLISHERS
47 CHURCH AVENUE, KENTVILLE, NS B4N 2M7
Literary Outfitters & Cultural Wilderness Guides.